Cover: Author on right. Her sister Helen on left.

Circa 1959

Cover Design: Ginny Pomaro

By Mary E. Lally

To Marty warmest Regards, Penance

To AMANDA You are the Best. Peace. Much Love, Mary 2012

Order this book online at www.trafford.com/06-1464
or email orders@trafford.com

Most Trafford titles are also available at major online book retailers.

Note for Librarians: A cataloguing record for this book is available from Library
and Archives Canada at www.collectionscanada.ca/amicus/index-e.html

Printed in Victoria, BC, Canada.

ISBN: 978-1-4120-9708-6

*We at Trafford believe that it is the responsibility of us all, as both individuals
and corporations, to make choices that are environmentally and socially sound.
You, in turn, are supporting this responsible conduct each time you purchase a
Trafford book, or make use of our publishing services. To find out how you are
helping, please visit www.trafford.com/responsiblepublishing.html*

*Our mission is to efficiently provide the world's finest, most comprehensive
book publishing service, enabling every author to experience success.
To find out how to publish your book, your way, and have it available
worldwide, visit us online at www.trafford.com/10510*

 www.trafford.com

North America & international
toll-free: 1 888 232 4444 (USA & Canada)
phone: 250 383 6864 ♦ fax: 250 383 6804 ♦ email: info@trafford.com

The United Kingdom & Europe
phone: +44 (0)1865 722 113 ♦ local rate: 0845 230 9601
facsimile: +44 (0)1865 722 868 ♦ email: info.uk@trafford.com

10 9 8 7 6 5 4 3 2

"All that I am, or hope to be, I owe to my angel mother."
~Abraham Lincoln

One of the toughest experiences you can go through is losing a loved one. When they pass on, a part of you goes along with them. Most of us eventually stop celebrating their soul due to the unwanted pain that it can bring. In her newest book, *Thirty Nine Cents*, Mary E. Lally refuses to quiet her mother's spirit. She is determined to carry on Elizabeth's legacy and celebrate her wondrous life.

In those last few weeks, Elizabeth and Mary become more than a mother and daughter, they became soul mates. The bond they formed was so powerful that it transcends even death. With charm, humor, wit and wisdom, Mary takes you through the stages of her grief and how she is able to continue on her mortal journey with her angel "Elizabeth" guiding her path along the way. Mary learns that by honoring their past, celebrating the precious months they were able to reconnect and finding how to forgive, she ultimately starts to discover her inner peace.

Mary E. Lally is a strong and brave woman teaching us the meaning of compassion and showing us all that in times of great anguish and despair, there is always a rainbow shining above. The key is to be looking up long enough to find it.

In Love,
Mary Sierra

This writing of sorts is dedicated to the Molly Malloy's' of the world. In times of great pain, adversity and loss they are able to pick up the pieces and move on with poise, grace and strength. To "my Mary" who I am sure will one day be sitting next to me saying, "Damn that was fun." To my cousin Stevee who has a beauty both inside and out, that only God and the Irish could have created. This is also dedicated to my mom who finally had the most precious of coins in her empty change purse, thirty-nine cents. To Pat Quigley who saw me through a window at the end of my journey and opened the door, to allow me the greatest gift my mother could have ever left me.

I would also like to dedicate this to anyone who has lost, and thought they would never recover. In my own personal battle with mourning the loss of my mother it was both a torment and a triumph. The torment was the loss of the only woman I am privileged to call mom. The triumph was surviving the mourning. I spent days on the couch, hours in tears, and weeks in indelible sadness. Time and friends healed my deeply gashed heart and aching besieged soul. Time in its infinite wisdom brought new days, sometimes welcomed with opened arms, sometimes looked upon with dread. There was no immediate healing. No matter how I wished for the pain to dissipate, it lingered. It only left in due time. A blessing of it's own I suppose.

I have been blessed with people in my life who know how it is. No one pushed me, offered clichés, or gave me up for lost. People allowed me hugs, silence and smiles. As I said in "Dear Elizabeth", when your mother passes on nothing seems the same. no phone calls, no visits, no lively spats. Chasing memories takes on a whole new meaning. I still miss Betty-Boop. I pray I always will. I have learned much in the few years since she's gone, and it was all because of her. Hey, who knew!

Peace to you always,

Mary

For Augusta

She never really saw my face.

She knew me for my shadow and loved me just the same….

For Her Daughters Roz &Fran

There is nothing more difficult than the time you must make the decision to grow up without hesitation, without reservation. It is a timeframe you will carry long into the ages that you pass in time. It is perhaps the greatest moment of your life. You must stand tall.

For it is then that you will be able to look to the heavens, as no other time and be grateful for the moment, for it only comes once in a lifetime…

*"WHEN YOU WALK THROUGH A STORM HOLD YOU HEAD UP HIGH
AND DON'T BE AFRAID OF THE DARK. AT THE END OF THE STORM IS A
GOLDEN SKY AND THE SWEET SILVER SONG OF A LARK,.. WALK ON,..
WITH HOPE IN YOUR HEART AND.. . .*

("YOU'LL NEVER WALK ALONE")

Rogers & Hammerstenn

I

Hey mom, it's me. As if you didn't know. I've

been thinking about you an awful lot lately and

wanted to let you know things are pretty okay. It has

been a long year and then some, without you.

Something happened deep inside of me the day you

left. Sometimes I think I can put my finger on it, and

sometimes I can't.

When all was said and done, and all the

whispering ended, I came back to my little apartment

far away from the place I once called home. Life

appeared before me in slow motion. Judy was by my side. She came immediately.

No questions. She was there in what seemed to be an instant. True friendship; it's a wonderful thing. Judy knew how to be, and when to be, and even knew when not to be. She seemed to understand every moment. My healing began when she walked into the wake. Both you and dad were impressed with my friends, later on in my life. And I do emphasize later on. Years past, more than once, both you and dad at one time or another lay in wait to pounce on what you believed to be an unscrupulous friend of mine. Did it ever occur to you guys that their parents felt the same way about me? In this life I am truly blessed with the most wonderful friends. I could ask for no better.

In every corner of the large crowd at our final farewell to you, I was sheltered by an umbrella of friends amassed from many years of learning. God has been good to me.

"Get your elbows off the table"

It took some time before I could find any space in my heart that didn't seem to be in unbearable anguish. When you died, life, as I knew it would be changed forever. For the first days after the dust settled, even breathing seemed to be a great effort.

Heavy sigh had a whole new meaning to me. My newfound friend was gone, and so was my mother, the woman who lived her life in the shadows of others' dreams. I had so much fun with you. Who could have thought that you and I would make it through what we made it through, without killing each other? You and I loving each other in the end seemed so easy, and yet we spent a lifetime daring each other about it. Never say never. I am amazed at how much "never" I am able to handle in my life. I never thought I could ever make it through your leaving. Throughout my life, I dreaded the thought of your dying. When it came to the real thing, I became someone I hardly knew.

"Don't sit on the edge of the couch"

I suppose the executioner throwing me out of the house was a good thing in a way. I had to drive my car through a flood of tears while trying to find a place to stay so I wouldn't have to drive so far in the dark and on my own.

Once again my friends came through for me. But his throwing me out forced me through the most challenging "never" of my mortal life. I was so mad at him, I forgot for a time, how sad I was about losing

10

you. I even pulled to the side of the road at one point, closed the windows, and screamed. I hurt my throat. At another time in my life, I would have been a lunatic with some irresponsible act to repent for. On this day in my life, I had the awesome responsibility of being responsible to both you and me together, for one last time. Geez, you know mom, it was like floating through the air those first weeks without you. Segments of moments kept racing through my mind. There seemed to be so many things running into each other. Crying, was a given. At any moment. Life had just happened to me. The part of life that has changed me for the remainder of my mortal being .

"Sit up straight"

When you left, "your house" went with you. I miss it. I just wanted to be in there once more. To sit in the living room and look out to the street. I wanted to walk through to the back porch, and sit with you for nine innings in the summer and four quarters in the winter. I wanted to go up to the bedroom where I slept with my three sisters and younger brother, long before adulthood made mountains out of molehills. I wanted to sit at your kitchen table with my coffee and watch you do the crossword thru your store bought half peepers. I would have been happy to be in the house alone, just for an hour. To pass through all the rooms where I knew every nook and cranny. Just to be in there to feel you around me one more time. To listen to the sounds of the secrets those tired walls held. Just to be home again.

"Don't talk with your mouth full"

I was never to travel through the abyss of memories the way I wanted; rather I was left to imagine what it looked like without you. I wanted to go up in the attic and bang my head on that low

ceiling for the millionth time. I wanted to walk

through every door once more. Every door in your

house had it's own special squeak, the cellar door, the

bathroom door, your bedroom door, remember? And

the doorknobs, remember when daddy painted them

all a different color? They were very cool colors. You

never did kill him for that. He lived long enough to

start fifty different projects and finish none of them.

When you think about it mom he did get his bit of

shanty Irish in, in his own little ways. Like the

bedroom window that was held open in the blazing

hot summers by a stick for forty years. The lock on

the front door: when you wanted to go out, you

locked it from the inside, and went out the back door,

leaving it unlocked so you could get back in. Yet the

toy monkey who rode across the back -porch ceiling

on fishing line, never fell off his bicycle. Dad had his

priorities. Apparently the monkey was one of them. There were so many reasons I wanted to go back and see your beloved house again. I wanted to feel it. Funny thing about your house. From moment to moment one never knew what they were going to feel like. There was always so much going on all the time.

"It's liver, it's good for you and you better eat it"

When we were little, someone always had a fishhook in his or her finger, or a wooden splinter in his or her tootsie. Of course there was always someone fighting with someone. Daddy would watch the "Munsters" or pretended to be sleeping on the couch, and you would be yelling to someone to stir the spaghetti while the water boiled all over the place. I remember being small enough to hide in the cubby closet in the dining room. I also remember getting hell for not being able to get out of it, when you screamed to get out of it. I don't know if I was more scared about being stuck in it or that I was scared about you yelling at me for being stuck. Whatever, I lived to talk about it to this day. Even that door had it's own special sound when you opened it. And the stuff you had in it later on in years, every little gadget imaginable. Cool. Wish I had a nickel for every time I heard you say "it's always something". How boring it would have been any other way. Besides, you might have accidentally killed one of us, just out of boredom.

"Wait till daddy gets home"

It blows my mind how much I miss you. I know in my life I will never again feel such emptiness as I feel in the vast space where you once belonged, both inside and outside my life. I get off the couch something like you used to. It used to take you two or three push offs before centrifugal force pushed you upright. It takes me two push offs. You were good though, once you got up your knees cracked, you did a two-step and you were off to wherever.

"What time is it?

Your house was always my home. Even with all the running away I did, I always had your house to come home to. God, mom I just wanted to be in it once more. I have this never-ending wonder about it. No matter what, I felt safe there. I felt safe with you, never really realizing that until I watched you leave. There were people everywhere hours after you left. Yet I never felt more alone in my entire life. Your house, the house we shared together for a million moments before you left, sounded hollow to me now. The deep voices of the police officers, who were so kind, seemed to echo as they spoke quietly and respectfully to us. The only house left on that part of Brooklyn Avenue was changed forever.

"Honey, your shoes are on the wrong feet"

Your mother and father who once raised chickens in the backayard were gone, daddy who tried desperately for shanty Irish was waiting for you, and you who loved that house no matter what it did or didn't have, had to leave. We were the losers. All the people who had fond memories of your house way back when, are now gone. We will never again hear the stories of the chickens and the wayward that found a soft bed to sleep in. There is no one to reminisce of one great party or another. Some amazing stories, you just couldn't make stuff up.

"Is mommy ever coming home?"

When you and your house left, I lost a part of my heart that held so much of my years. You knew me my entire life. There is no other soul that can claim that somewhat scary thought. I want you to tell me again about how little I was when I was born. I want you to tell me again about how things were for you guys when you lived in the Bronx and Long Beach. I want you to tell stories about what it was like to have so many little kids underfoot every moment of your life. I want to hear how you cooked up food enough to feed the entire brood on two dollars and one trip to Bohack's. You could make spaghetti more different ways than anyone else in the world.

Remember the time you and dad got a Navy cookbook and made five hundred biscuits. I will never forget the time you made those ugly pickles. They stunk to high heaven. They were in jars everywhere, including the bathroom closet. What were you thinking? You know mom, when you used to talk about the old days, it was so easy to picture it. I can't picture it anymore, not without your voice to take me there.

"Hurry up they're home"

I've heard you yell to me ten or more times,"Get your dead ass off the couch and stop crying or I'll give you something to cry about". I'd stop crying, but for a while there I stayed on the couch. I was just so tired. You and I lived through some "wish I hadn't done that" sort of stuff in our lifetime together, but your leaving sent me solo, into a world of unknown fear. A huge fear. Death is such a huge thing. I keep waiting for it to be over, but it doesn't end. It just keeps on going. No matter how I wish you were coming home to be in your house again you're not, but the memories of you hold fast.

Perhaps the greatest gift of death is the treasure of the memories we are given. And we can relive them anytime and anywhere we want. Such a wonderful freedom. Sometimes I search for memories of you. Trying real hard to think of something from one time or another. Sometimes it tunes in fuzzy, sometimes as clear as the day it happened. And then there are those times when a song brings me to tears, or I see your favorite cookie at the grocery, or I hear of Valley Stream. No matter what it be, it's a keeper. Through choice, I have trinkets of memories in carefully selected places throughout my apartment. I need those things to be there, out in the open. It doesn't make me sad to see those things. It almost always brings me to a memory of some sort. Either that or I just trip over it.

"Jiggle the handle"

On a recent very cold rainy winter day I went with Sean, Terry and the kids to make sure everything on your stone was spelled right before they put it in the ground (I guess Sean and Terry never knew, or they forgot that you never let me forget that I spelled Elizabeth, my middle name wrong, while in the third grade, on an intelligence test no less!), it knocked me into such a strange reality. There written in beautiful dark green marble was yours and dad's names written in stone. No erasing. The finality of it all, rested heavily on my heart. I touched my fingers to the stone, and ran my

21

fingers quickly over your name. It was at that instant that I stopped dead. Yep, this was yours, no doubt about it. In the pouring winter rain, on the beautiful stone that Sean and Terry had picked out for all you guys, a bird had left its mark. And quite a mark it was. The more things change, the more they stay the same.

Everything must have been spelled right. I don't remember them asking me. I just remember standing there on that cold winters day. Reading those words through my tears. Those words on a beautiful marble stone, etched with symbols of our Irish heritage. This striking stone, it bore the names of the people who were precious to me here on this earth and who were now in the hands of God, finally at peace. Sean called when the stone was finally in place.

"What, did you say"..?!!!!!!

22

The long winter made it seem like forever before the stone was put in. I didn't mind the wait. It was just one more finality that I was dreading in this process of mourning you. Mom, ya know this growing up thing, it just seems to be taking such a long time. So many times I want to call you and ask you something, or tell you something. So many times since you left I want to look across your kitchen table and say "Betty Boop", "What the----." I do it in my heart, which is always chasing after a memory of you, from one time or another. But you know Betty Boop, it's just not the same.

"Daddy's gonna kill you"

I find myself going to the docks a lot. Not the ones in Woodmere where you used to go with daddy, but out here by me in Northport. Daddy used to love to do that, you just went because it got you out of the house. Although later on, the both of you got a kick out of it. Sometimes the peace of the water's painted reflections takes me back in time. Do you remember the time I threw up in daddy's rowboat? That was the first time I ever heard him say that Jesus H. Christ thing he used to say. He couldn't figure out why I didn't put my head over the side and how I could possibly be sick tied to the dock. He would have gone on yelling, but he had the gags. I remember the fishhook in my thumb. He never yelled. He just kept looking at you shaking his head. I think on that one all he did was ask me to hold his fishing pole. I guess I didn't know it was loaded.

"And don't come down till I say so"

Sean has named me "Lucky Star", and with good reason as you know. Daddy, the water and I never really did get along. At least not when the three of us were together. There was that sailboat thing. I thought it was pretty cool flying with the wind. I never thought of how we would get back. The best was the time in Mystic Connecticut. There was a rope swing over the creek. He told me to try it, I didn't think it was a good idea, but tried it anyway. I took off on the rope, never let go over the water and daddy went flying on his ass trying to get out the path of my return flight.

"Get upstairs right now"

I held on to that rope till it stopped dead. I was not letting go for anything. Man, daddy's eyes were watering by this time. "Let go of the goddamn rope"!!!! I didn't answer. "Mary honey let go of the rope, it's only water". I let myself slide down the rope, ripping the hell out of my hands. The water

25

was not the issue. He was never going to let me live it down, not a chance. It was in that very place that dad and a chipmunk shared a can of peanuts. Daddy made a line of peanuts across the table then came and sat in the camper. He did it everyday. One day it was just he and the chipmunk sitting at the table. When we left, daddy left the chipmunk a whole can of peanuts. You missed that trip.

"What do mean, you forgot."

Remember how you hated camping? On our first trip you made daddy bring you all the way home from Rhode Island. You remember that place where Sean and Mike ended up on the post card. We were not meant to camp as a family. Daddy learned that the hard way. His way to finally camp in peace was to purchase the smallest pick-up truck manufactured on this earth.

He was nuts, wasn't he? That explains it. All along I thought it was you who was nuts. You taught me much about mothers and God getting blamed for so much. You wondered why it could never be the wacko kids fault. How come the kid was never some kind of deviant? It was always the mother's and God's fault. When mothers were getting blamed for everything, you were flipping your wig. It was you who opened my eyes to all the stuff you as a mother got blamed for. And it was you who always reminded me of the fact that you were going to win no matter what. Thank God. And thank you Jesus for the really short nun who could pull three hairs at a time, on my still developing head, hence making me do what ever it was she wanted me to do. In all honesty if it weren't for those nuns who had the ability to pull one hair or three at a time, I wouldn't be writing you this letter. I know you know that mom. We were going to get educated-beaten just as you did, come hell or high water. Remember the day you got three of us all spruced up, dresses and all. Poor daddy dragged us across the highway under the railroad trestle, when someone went ass over teakettle in their best clothes through an icy puddle. Didn't much matter to you though because, we still got to meet that nun that very day, who had the power to approve or disapprove of who or what stood before her. She approved and then lived to regret it, I am certain.

"What do you mean you don't know."

Discipline, it's a wonderful thing. You won with the wooden spoons, most of the nuns left the convent, and I am not serving time and still breathing last time

I checked. Think about it mom, with all the minor mishaps I encountered and all the times you wanted to kill me, I turned out okay. You even told me that. And in that instant, I felt warm all over. I never felt more loved at any other time in my life as I did when you took my hands kissed them and told me you loved me. Remember it was the last time in this earthly life that we talked. It is treasured in my heart as clear as the day you left. Life changes in instants. I thought about that a lot after the accident. More so after you left. In the instant when you took my hands I felt what I had wanted so much to feel throughout my entire life. Such peace. Such solace. Thank you.

"It's her turn, I did it last time."

After that last incident at your house, I chose to make myself unavailable to any of the so-called family meetings that the executioner called. He

29

always called them through someone else. I never got

the lanterns that hung over the fireplace. I never got

the ones I left to replace them either. I wanted them

because they were grama's, and no one on earth knew

if they worked or not. It was always guess work

when you hit the switch as to whether you would

blow a fuse or set the house on fire. Why the lot of

them just couldn't take them out and put up the

replacements was beyond me. It was too much work

I was told. Everything in that house was too much

work what the hell more could two lanterns, that a

boyfriend of grama's got from some fancy hotel in the

city do to increase the baloney. Well, apparently a

whole lot cause I came out empty on that one. Gra

loved those. Some ole flame from eons of time ago

was in construction and got them for her. I can't

recall the name of the hotel in New York City. I

remember she used to smile when she spoke of him and the lanterns. At least I have the stories.

"Who told you, you could do that?"

You told me the others were afraid that if I stayed in your house that I wouldn't leave after your time had come for you to leave. You also said I could stay there until all the formalities were done, Helen could too if need be. But the pea brain took care of that. He claimed he was afraid of wild parties. I just wanted to lie in your bed once more. I wanted to sit at your memory worn kitchen table with the light about the stove casting soft shadows around the room where life once took center stage. I wanted to feel you across the back porch.

"I'm not going". "You are if I say your going"

After all that time we had together, I just wanted
time to say goodbye to the rooms in your house that
sheltered me from harm and held me in punishment.
Every room had a million stories, and thirty coats of
Sears paint. Remember the time Helen and I were
being "jailed" in our room and one of my friends tied
a bag of goodies to the string we had dropped out the
window. I thought we had it made until daddy's arm
came out the kitchen window, grabbed the bag and
took string and all back into the kitchen. My friend
took off, and Helen and I waited for the death threat
to come thru the bedroom door. It never came, which
was worse. Waiting for daddy that day, and his
never coming up to our room was worse than
anything. Helen and I cry laughing each and every
time we chase that memory. I just can't remember
which thing we had done to earn a week in our room.
I think he even took my stereo that time. It couldn't

have been the liquor in the coke bottle thing with Pam, because I remember dad couldn't even send her home because she lived with us. Whatever it was we did do, apparently the punishment worked, and we all lived through it.

"If you can't find something nice to say about someone than don't say anything at all'

It's pretty amazing what we live through, when we think so hard that we won't. All the time we were together, in the back of my mind was always, the ending of us together. I was petrified. You were leaving. I was watching you leave, and you were living your demise. I made my way through it, and in my heart and soul I have you, and in a way mom, you made it too. You were able to say goodbye to your mortal life. You not only made it, but you are a winner.

In your life you were a winner, you just didn't know it, and I like you with others didn't know the winner you were. You know mom, you and I had a lot of support on our journey. People were pretty cool. But there were just sometimes that no matter what someone said, I just felt so alone, so afraid. And I know you did too. There were days when your silence was much louder than other days. Your face said a lot. For me sometimes it was just leave me the hell alone, don't say anything, just shut up. Just because. Words didn't seem to do anything to what I was feeling. They didn't seem to help, but they didn't hurt either. I just felt like I wanted quiet.

When people talked I felt like I couldn't see where I was going. I was doing what I was doing, not having a clue, exactly what it was I was trying to do. People were really wonderful, truly. But mom your leaving was the greatest permeation of loneliness I will ever experience. You were always there for any other loss I had in my life. You were there when Gra died, and when dad died. But when you left there was no one there. No one Betty Boop could fill your shoes. There seemed to be this abyss of emptiness all around me. My best friends were at my side immediately upon hearing that your extraordinary journey had reached its ultimate ebb. And yet there bold, as all hell was that vast emptiness that I know I shall only feel once, in this mortal life.

"Stop cryin' or I'll give you somethin' to cry about"

One thing I learned in our time together was that God sent me to you for more reasons than you and I shall ever know. I mean mom think about it. How many times did you tell me that things happened for a reason. I was sent to make you nuts. You and I worked hard at our given roles. I spent my childhood thinking I was tougher than you, and you spent my childhood proving it was you who was the tougher of the two of us, hands down. Never would you prove that point more than when I traveled with you on your precious, arduous journey, home. I would give the shadow of my soul to walk you up those fourteen steps, just once more. I think of those trips up the stairs every now and then, and it's not so scary as they were when we walked together. Now I cherish the bursts of moments that are still fresh in my mind. I implore my memory to allow me to keep you at a moments notice. Sometimes without a glimmer I can feel the tears before I can envision the thought. And Betty Boop that's okay too.

"Leave your sister alone. And that goes for you too."

I have not yet figured out how to "grow up" and not feel orphaned. We all know I can't run, but there are times when I feel like I am a child running into yours or daddy's legs. I remember running towards you when I was little, you were always holding someone or something in your arms, so your legs were usually the target. Nine out of ten times someone or myself stepped on your forever-bad big toe, or hit daddy in the family jewels. Now that I think about it, did we ever have a Kodak moment in our house? I never really thought about growing up until after you left. I hate just having me to answer to. I don't have to explain anything to anyone, anymore. There is no one who has the right to ask me questions like you did. Not that you ever asked me questions that I couldn't answer. You weren't real nosy ever. I even answered questions you never asked, just to be safe.

"Stop trying to erase your beautiful freckles. Remember a face

without freckles is like a sky without stars"

There is no one any more that I am afraid of.

And when I say afraid it's not of you but what you

would think of me if I did something questionable. I

hated it when I hurt you in one way or another. The

respect I worked at towards you over the years, you

deserved. There is no one to make me feel like a

forty-nine year old child. Ya know mom you still

scared the crap out of me when you yelled, right up

until you left. When you left, a secret secure feeling

that must have been there all along and I didn't even

know it, became lost. This whole different picture

appeared in my heart, and it hurt. It scared me. It

saddened me.

Dad's version of grace before meals: "Good bread, good

meat, good God let's eat"

I am not exactly sure how to describe to you my first year after you left. Possibly a blur. Yeah that's it. Blur after blur. You know mom it's so much easier to cry than it is to try not to cry. I know you hated it, but I 've got to tell you that crying for you and me was all I could do for a couple of weeks. It seemed that the slightest sound brought me into reality. And then it was boo hoo for eons of tears. At times my tears felt so heavy. All the crying I tried to hide from you during the journey must have found its path.

"Where's your brother"... ... "How'd he get up there?"

At times it's as though I look for you. Like on the street or in a car, I know it sounds strange but I feel like I look for you. I keep thinking yes, maybe I will see you again, if I just keeping looking in all the right places it might really happen. It's not all the time, just once in a while. I don't really know what I would do if I should and you. First, I guess I would duck, just in case. But you know what mom; I don't think I've done anything since you left, which would make me need to duck. The job thing I know, but mom, I get so tired in my brain so early in the day. That hamster, he falls off his wheel much quicker now. But I do try and do the right thing all the time... I think I'm going to duck. My idea of the right thing and your idea of the right thing might be a little different now. I pretty much always agreed with you when you were standing within spoon's length, but once at a safe distance I tested the waters with my own ideas. I think I spent my entire adolescence wishing I hadn't tested the waters. Not that you and daddy were always right or anything like that, but... Well you guys might have been right some of the time. You have to admit mom, there were times that you were sort of dumb about some things. I guess it was safer for you not to know something. Daddy on the other hand, had the street smarts. He caught us at the damnedest things, and with that "Wadda ya think, I was never a kid, ya dopey kid ya." I hated it when he said that. He was more of a kid than we were. Except when he looked six feet tall and telling me to get up to my room.

"If I ever find out who, I didn't do it is"

I do not wish to go back to my youth in your house, just back to our time together. I am very lucky to have had you for the time I did. I do not wish to see you because I regret anything or to make up for anything rather to just be with you and create more of what we had before you left. Like calling you,

hanging out with you doing our laundry. I miss you

telling me to talk louder. I miss making a face. I miss

you catching me make that face. I miss closed caption

Spanish TV. Man I'm getting brave aren't, I? Your

house was such a huge part of my life. Sean's too. No

one seemed to get the fact that he and I were the only

two that had a key to your house. At least when you

started locking the door that is. He and I spent the

most time there, and it was Sean and I who just

wanted to go back and breathe in what would never

be the same to us ever again in our lives. It was Sean

and I who could see things in that house that the

others could never understand, both good and bad. I

sometimes think Irene could too, but she would never

admit to it. Sean's first stop when ever he came in

was to check the top of the fireplace for mail, check

the fridge and then kiss you hello. Except when you

were sitting in one of your daydreaming chairs in the living room. Then he kissed you first. Funny, from those chairs, you could watch the world go by on the streets outside, warm and cozy in the winter and cool in the summer. You'd keep a close eye on Sean when he was cutting the grass out front, waving to him once in a while. I have one of those chairs and Sean has the other.

"How many times do I have to tell you"?

This second year is a killer. Numbness is definitely a safe thing to have the first year after you lose a pal. Numbness came later on. Much after reality set in. Reality set in, immediately. There was no shock at your leaving. There was no screaming. Reality was right there with you, Sean and me. It was the boldest reality of my life. All the weeks before that moment, I was heading full blast. Straight into the moment. When the moment came, it came with a profound silence that felt deafening. This was what it felt like to have your heart break. Nothing could ever feel like this to me again. The first year I went through all the first's without you. Christmas and football were the worst. I bawled like a baby on opening day of the Jets game. I was invited out that day and I couldn't go cause I couldn't stop crying. I let Christmas just pass by. I stayed home. I wanted to. I just let it go by. Probably the first time in my life I ever did that. Even while I was in rehab I celebrated Christmas. But not the year you left.

"Close the god damn door I'm not heating the neighborhood"

Christmas time in your house later on was pretty cool. Your tree had the neatest little ornaments, and you could pretty much remember where each one came from. Mostly from when daddy was still here and you two would go shopping. The amazing thing about your tree later on was that it wasn't held up straight by fishing line anymore. Every year dad was alive he grunted and groaned with the "damn tree" trying to get it to stay upright. The fishing line ran the length of the porch ceiling, and the tree usually stayed up. Years before it always came down for one reason or another. It was either a kid, a pet, or a wayward breeze, that would cause the tree to fall. I remember those teeny weenie little pieces of glass from those ornaments that met their demise on the porch floor. Bet those ornaments would be worth a small fortune today. Then daddy discovered fishing line, when he had nothing else. It was hardly noticeable, it held the tree up, and he could leave the remnants hang in the porch for years and you would never see them. Remember the time the tree was too tall for the ceiling and he cut the top off? Holey moley were you mad.

"Man is daddy mad at you"!

The lights were a whole different fiasco. He always got some imp to walk the wire around while he threw the light strand hoping all the while it would land on a branch. It took many years before fuses didn't blow when you plugged the tree in for the first time. I remember Helen and I trying to put Christmas lights up on the front of the house. It was bitter cold. We plugged them in while the tree was plugged in and blew everything. Pretty cool. At least we thought so. There's no such thing as fuses anymore are there? Then there was you with that damn tinsel. One thousand strands per box and you were determined that they were not to be thrown on in bunches, rather laid on branches one at a time so

46

they hung like fake icicles should hang. When you weren't looking we threw as many as we could.

"Make sure you wash behind your ears"

I can still hear the velvety tone of your voice when you use to sedate us with "Listen my children and you shall hear the midnight ride of Paul Revere", or "T'was the night before Christmas and all through the house not a creature was stirring not even a mouse"... I remember being mesmerized by both those readings. My favorite part was when the guy hears the hooves of the reindeer on his roof and jumped out of bed. By the way you used to read it, it sounded like it could have happened at our house. Remember when I was a sugarplum in the first grade? I don't. I just remember you told me and I was just wondering if you still remembered it. Me a sugarplum. It had to be because in those days, a girl just couldn't play a reindeer.

Every day since you left is a first. Every day there is a new reason for me to realize you're not here anymore. It's not always a heavy-duty reason; sometimes it's just a small twinkle of a thought. The times I really feel it is when I know you would know the answer to something I needed to know. Like how to get the squeak out of my sneakers. Or who built the Brooklyn Bridge and how long did it take. I know you would know the answers. As I write you I am having trouble with squeaky sneakers. You would have some simple answer to the squeak. From there we could go back in time to some other place. You would tell me something that they used to do in the "olden days" that still worked these days. I liked to listen when you talked about the "olden days". You were no angel in your olden days. Daddy always said the "nut don't fall far from the tree". I'm still not sure if he meant I was a nut because I fell from his tree or because I fell from your tree. Usually, according to daddy, I was your daughter when I did something mischievous and his daughter when I did something right. But remember mom he always had to come and get me when I ran away.

"Whose turn is it to empty the dishwasher"?

My "olden days", are not old yet. I wish I could share my not so olden days with you. I know you are with me in spirit. But I'd like to talk about fun stuff and laugh my head off with you. Like the time dad, you and I were lost for what seemed to be hours. Dad finally pulled into a gas station and asked for directions. You were so proud of him for doing it.

You couldn't hear the man making his directional sounds. I was crying laughing in the back seat. The man daddy asked, was a deaf mute. I was not laughing at the man, rather I was laughing at the thought that this could only happen to daddy. Daddy stood there shaking his head like he could understand this man's attempt at vocalism, listened politely, got in the car and off we went, passing the same restaurant for the third time. There are so many things I want to tell you about. I want so much to hear you laugh again. It was so cool getting to know you. That was perhaps the greatest gift. Learning, knowing, no more guessing. Honesty was all we had. The most honest thing in living is the dying, and it was right there with us, with every quickened breath we took, and every tear I tried not to cry. But you know mom it was the first time in our lives together that I wasn't running from you and you weren't chasing after me. And it wasn't even boring. Who knew.

"Zipper your coat, where's your other mitten?"

With twenty one percent of the family (Gra's in there) looking down from up above, and fifty percent of the family looking down their noses and not speaking with me I have made some major adjustments to my address book. I no longer have one. I know you are not liking it one bit. But it's really okay.

"If I ever hear you say that again I'm gonna wash your mouth out with soap. Do you hear me"?

Mom, it took me a long time to get to where I am now. Some people would say I am nowhere. Those people can no longer touch me.

51

Over the years I have seen things in people that were both good and bad. I have seen ugly be more beautiful than anything I had ever witnessed, and I have seen beauty turn to winter's scorn. I walked quietly, until now. Watching you fight death gave me an unimaginable will of courage. I am okay without them. My life is very peaceful. I hope you understand. I can now sometimes laugh when I am in some great feeling of despair and I can cry tears of joy, when something that I see or feel great about appears before my eyes and in my heart. I did not get to this point on my own. It must be a master plan mom, because the way it all happened is amazing. The timing for the pieces to fall into place was near perfect. And most of the things that happened, we had no control over: the accident, the cancer, the dying and some of the living. (Are you giving me one of those what the hell are you talking about looks? I can feel it) People can say what they want about why I stayed with you till the end. I had no agenda. I was not making up to you for something I had done in the past. (It would take us two lifetimes together for me to do that.) I was there because you are my mother. I was there to do what ever you wanted done at any given moment. We both know that what we did together wasn't easy. But we did it, and pretty well I might add. You knew it too. It was like I could feel that from you in that moment you took my hands and told me you loved me. By the way I have recently learned that you were not the only wooden spoon wielding mother of the fifties and sixties. It seems Italian mothers not only used the wooden spoon but they threw their shoe too!

"Who drank all the milk?"

I am not angry that you are gone. Just very, very sad. I never got angry about it. There was no justifiable reason to be angry. You had big cancer and there were no choices. God had set His date for you to go home. I was too scared all the time to get angry. There was no time to get angry. Just time to catch the whispers of sadness that permeated meekly into our final days together.

"Go ask your mother "." I did."
She said to ask you"

In the time that has passed since you left, life outside the living room and kitchen windows has gone on. Not that I witnessed it, but I tried with all my heart to remember looking out your kitchen window and watching you look out the living room window. I used to wonder why we went inside to look out the window. Lifetimes passed by your house windows. On the outside the same families passed by your house every Sunday at the same time of morning for years. We always had a famous landmark to use when giving directions to your house. Changes occurred all around us. You remembered the changes from eons ago. I could remember them wrecking the old firehouse, which happened in '57. For all those years what other neighborhood kids we did have, came and went. We weren't going anywhere. When we had no other kids to fight with, we fought with each other. We built forts in the backayard. We formed bands and pretended to be everywhere except where we really were. We annoyed the good humor man into early retirement, and kept Wetson's in business for a year after it's true demise. We floated our imaginations down the running puddles in front of your house before Brooklyn Avenue became such a busy street. We had the greatest games of stickball off the wall of the yellow building. We made snow forts in the firehouse parking lot and slid down the hill in Reingold beer trays. Remember the day I broke my nose climbing the fence. I'll never forget it. We watched fireworks on the fourth of July from the front steps for years until the trees got too high. And good old Gene's block. His mother made the greatest cookies and she always had some for us. All we had to do was knock on her door or sit on the curb outside her house and she would give us one.

"And don't give me any of your lip!"

So many lives became stories just within that somewhat square of a neighborhood we grew up in.

And what a square it was. Your legacy was the beginning and the ending of that square. Your life there on Brooklyn Avenue touched so many lives, in so many ways. It was evident when we laid you and dad to rest, on that warm August morning. So many came to say goodbye to a part of their childhood, so many of them, mom. I have to tell you that I completely forgot about daddy. I mean the last time I paid much attention to where he was, was when you wanted me to dust the top of the china closet and we had to move him. That was the fastest dust job I ever did. I was okay that he was up there and I could stop by and give him a box of Tipperillos, but the thought that I had to pick him up was another thing. You patted the top of the box, like you used to pat him on the top of his baldhead, handed me back the box and walked away. I couldn't move. I was so afraid of dropping him, I froze for a minute. I had visions of daddy being vacuumed up off the dining room floor if I dropped the box.

Things with you got serious soon after that. I just never thought about him up there on the china closet. So on that warm August day I said goodbye to both you and dad for the last time. You and him together again, in peace, finally, I hope. I have my doubts though. The evening of the day you left, there was a humdinger of a storm. Driving home I kept thinking you must have met up with daddy or Grama. Either that or you just wanted everyone to know you were on your way. That storm, everyone talked about it. It scared the hell out of me.

"Offer it up for the souls in purgatory"

I wish we could have coffee again. Just so I could watch you from across the table doing the crossword. You amazed me with the clues you could get the answer to. It was the Latin you said. You remembered those nun's from Bishop McDonald in Brooklyn, and the Latin they drilled into your rebelling brain. You were good at Jeopardy too. It took me a long time before I could watch it again once you left. I still can't watch Mash. That music was playing when you left. I could hear it in the back round. But anyway, if we could have coffee once again I could at least bug you till you talked.

"Eat everything on your plate. There's kids starvin' in Europe"

No one can make jet fuel like you could. I come close but I can't afford that much coffee. I won't allow anyone to do anything better than you could. Besides there are just some things no one can make like your mother can make. The best grilled cheese came out of the cast iron frying pan, held to the heat with a half filled teakettle of water. The cheese from the U.S.D.A. that Grama traded off from somewhere. We used to call it welfare cheese. It was the best. Same thing for your fried spaghetti. I came home one night rather than wait on the open twenty four hours drive thru at White Castle with all the other hungry drunks and set the stove on fire trying to make fried spaghetti like yours. That was long ago, when I thought I could do anything and nothing would happen. There are still some thing's I know I do with a devil may care attitude. But those things I never did before, like not really care what people think of me. The devil may care attitude and thousands in school loans have been a wonderful boost to my confidence. Now instead of wanting to kill someone right off the bat, I give them a chance to explain.

You'd be proud of me right now. I know you would. I am so proud of you. I will always miss you. I make sure I miss you at some point every day because I sometimes get afraid that I will someday forget to miss you, and that would kill me. You left me with an unbelievable amount of strength. It is a strength I never had before. I don't ever want to let it go. I remember you said the worst thing about leaving was that you were going to miss everybody so much. Everybody misses you mom, everybody. This death thing, it never ends. It goes on for eternity. Part of my growing up was realizing that the death thing is truly for ever, perhaps one of the most painful aspects of life. Imagine a grain of sand that weighs, just about a ton. While you were dying, I was trying so hard to grow up. I was trying to be brave.

Trying with all my might to believe that you were going to a better place. I think when you love someone that much, you allow yourself to believe that they are truly going to a better place. After watching you I can't help but believe it is a better place. You were finally at peace. The peace radiated from you. It was amazing. You found it.

"There's no such thing as a boogey man, she's just tryin' to scare you, now go to bed"

I needed to believe that. I needed to convince myself that you were going to be all right wherever it was that you were going. I needed to know that nothing was going to hurt you anymore. I so wanted you to be safe from harm. I wanted you to be free from the dust bunnies that haunted you, your entire life. Just like you wanted to row your own boat to the end, I wanted you to soar. I often find myself remembering, and I am in awe of what you were able to do for yourself.

"That's not fair." "We'll see what's not fair."

When I think back about growing up with you as my mother I find myself wondering: how'd you do it? Yes I know Johnnie Walker had a part in it, and Gra helped a lot. You must have done something right though, no one went to jail and they all made it past puberty. I just made it to fifty. Those birthday blues were on the fringes of my days all that week. I wanted you to be here. I am the fourth of your children to turn fifty. In a dog's life, I am dead. I never thought about fifty. I remember you always made each their favorite food on their birthday. Mine was beef stew, but some how you always made that Mexican dish paella. I never asked. I loved it, but beef stew is still my favorite. I had hot dogs this year. Life is good.

"Someone took my underwear"

You and dad did a helluva job you know. It wasn't always fair on either side of the coin, not on yours and at times, not on ours. History it's a wonderful thing, you either can repeat it or, you can make it. I hope you realize how the odds were stacked against you and daddy. You pretty much had no history to follow. You made your own both good and bad. I wish you could have stood proud. I have seen people do a lot less than you did, and bask in the glory for eons. You had no idea how to bask in the glory. I can name a few specifics of when you glowed for one of us, but you never glowed for you. I try and glow for you every chance I get. Some don't understand why, and perhaps they never will.

"The fork goes on the left". "But I'm righty."

You never let me or anyone else glow about you when you were here. So now I can do all that I want. You deserve it. You should have gotten it while you were here. God knows you weren't perfect. You just thought you had to be, and because you knew you weren't, you couldn't love you the way you needed to. And because you couldn't love you the way you wanted, you couldn't love us in the way we thought you were supposed to love us. Some of us got over that, some didn't. If you just pretend to forgive, you can never forget. Gra was always into forgiveness. It is perhaps the greatest gift she could have bestowed on me. The hardest to understand, and at times an arduous challenge.

"Stand up straight"

You gave me so many gifts that I am aware of every day of my life. Did you ever think that the runt of the litter, who gave you the hardest run for your motherhood, would be by your side every step of the way as you journeyed towards everlasting Eden? Never in a million years, could I have ever imagined that what happened with us, could ever happen. I never thought about things like that. You taught me to be a survivor. I owe my life to you in more ways than one. I survived birth. I survived childhood with three older brothers and three younger sisters. I survived puberty, catholic school and you and daddy. Hee hee. I am ducking. I say you and daddy with a laugh because it's true. Sometimes I find myself in hysterics at the things we went through.

"Who took all the spoons out in the backyard

Still a mystery to me is how you caught me at the things you caught me at. The punishments were the most creative works of parenthood nestled within the walls of Brooklyn Avenue: saying you're sorry to a door after you slammed it, getting kitchen duty for forever, staying in your room for extended periods of time with no radio. That one wasn't bad because your chance of being alone for any length of time was zilch. You shared the room with three other sisters. No allowance. No surprise there, you rarely had it to give it to us anyway. Besides there was always daddy's pants hanging on the back of the bathroom door. One shake to hear a jingle, three shakes to get the pants to come off the hook and you had enough for a black and white and a Hershey bar. It was many years before I found out that I was not the only one raiding daddy's pockets. I was probably the only one who confessed to Father Hermann and had to say the entire rosary three times while on my knees. I got wise to that confessing thing pretty quick. If I had something better to do than kneel in church for the afternoon and beg for forgiveness I would save the worse sins for another time. That way I could get done with my Penance with time enough to goof off. Who Knew? Now I say the Rosary just for the heck of it, every day. Punishment. In those days it happened every time I turned around, or so it seemed. If it wasn't you and daddy it was some nun. Puberty and punishment should be studied more closely. If you ask me, puberty is a punishment. Ask any kid with acne.

"Turn off the light and go to bed already,

Happy Birthday! Doing any thing special to celebrate? As you know I am doing the usual. While you were here on earth you never wanted anything celebratory for your birthday I have pretty much kept to celebrating it with little fanfare. Year after year you begged me not to do anything big for your day. Your last birthday here, we had Dennis, Stevee and Emma over. Now we go to your favorite restaurant, Angelina's in Lynbrook. I bring that swell picture of you; order a scotch sour for you and we pig out. Paul comes and so does Kathleen. I hope you are looking out for Emma. She just left this week, so I don't know if you found her yet. Mom, when you do find her, please hold her close. Show her the ropes. Make sure she knows how much she was loved for her short stay here. She only made it to 63. She was so much like you, a brilliant mind, a kind heart and a weary soul.

So many lives changed dramatically forever. I pray that those closest to her find it in their hearts to know that God knew what He was doing when He called her home. Watching you gave me the strength to believe that there is a haven on the other side. It gave me the strength to believe that Emma has gone to that better place, where there is no more pain, neither physical nor emotional. I will miss Em tonight. She was such a fun person to be around. Look down on us tonight. I know I'll be looking up to you. Happy Birthday mom, I love you.

"Because I said so, that's why"

I stopped to see your house this week. It's been a while since I've been in that way. I always stop by your house when I do go in to Valley Stream. I try and look at it from a different view each time. I just want to take it all in. Sometimes I cry, sometimes I don't. I always think about something from times long ago. I try not to think about what happened when you left. This day I saw major changes and I wanted to just throw up. It appears that most of the crayon graffitied walls we as your children ever created and daddy ever painted over with Sears paint, lie broken with memories deceased, in the backayard. They must have gutted the whole house. It looks like the entire inside is now lying on the outside. Maybe they don't like almost shanty Irish. I remember after you left seeing broken pieces of two and three generations tossed in dumpsters. For some, it is always about their own convenience, the easiest way out the better. But like someone once said to me, "God don't like ugly, Mary". What happened was truly ugly. When I saw your beautiful brass bed lying atop other fragmented pieces of your life, shinning brightly in a filthy dumpster. I cried like a baby.

"Why did you do that"

That bed took up seventy-five-percent of your bedroom. It cradled you till the day before you left. It just never deserved to end up in a dumpster. Changing the sheets on that thing was always an adventure for me. I used to try and outsmart the fitted sheet by going top left corner to bottom right, somehow I always got nailed by the damn sheet. And there I would roll, and groan trying to get the fitted on the spot where it was supposed to go, with one hand. I figured if I lay on my stomach, it wouldn't be able to get away from me. Not only could it not get away from me, but also there was no slack for me to work with.

One time I started laughing and I couldn't stop. How the hell can you NOT be able to make a bed?

Mom, remember when you got us those "pull out beds"? I remember we used to rig them so the person getting into bed would collapse the bed as soon as they got on it. You knew we did it by the noise and then the kitchen light would blink. Pam was always an easy target for that. We got those beds after the bunk beds became such a safety issue. Who knew back then that kids would still fall out of bed, no matter how high up you put them.

Back then Daddy used to burn the trash. There were no dumpsters. Every kid in the neighborhood came the day daddy burned my "Johnnie Reb cannon". I can still see the black plastic melting in flames daddy fueled with other sentenced debris. I remember the Christmas I got it. I can still remember Joe's face when he found out it was for me and not him. I pulled that cannon everywhere I went. Mom, pieces of dreams of all of us were lying in the backayard in the rain. I thought I would be sick when I first caught sight of it. I had someone with me or I would have been. Sean says new owners, new memories. Just like I never thought what happened to you would happen, I never thought I would ever feel, what it would be like to be on the outside of our house wishing to look in. I guess I just always thought it would be ours. We were always supposed to be on the inside looking out. I never thought about seeing our funny, sad, sometimes crumbled lives, vanishing in dumpsters and drowning in the rains. Sure, some of it but, not so much of it.

"Because I'm the mommy"

Hey Mom remember the time they came to arrest you for an unpaid parking ticket? The officer who came to take you away was faced with four freckled faced kids boo hooing in the living room at the thought of him taking you away. It was a two-dollar parking ticket. The officer left without you, probably grateful he worked nights. You were the talk of the neighborhood kids for weeks. Not one kid could claim that the cops came to take their mother away, but we could. We were really proud of you. I think the penny meter is now a quarter.

"What in God's name did you do now"!!!!!!!!

Before I forget, thanks for looking out for us. We walked across the bridge, as you know. I know you think we were crazy to do it, but I think you knew that I was going, except for ice. I had been dreaming of walking across the Brooklyn Bridge since I was little and used to listen to Gra and you talk about it. I never gave it much thought though, after the accident. How would I ever get up those steps never mind walk across over the East River? Well more than a year ago, Helen asked me what was the one thing I always wanted to do. I was after all, turning fifty. (I knew you mom when you were fifty). We started planning for the walk across the Brooklyn Bridge. January was way too cold, so we decided on the first weekend in April. Who knew the weather predictions for that day would be three or more inches of rain and gale force winds. When all was said and done parts of New Jersey were underwater, trees were down all over, and parts of the Island were without electricity. There were nine lunatics scheduled to walk on that day. Everyone had the option of staying home. Those people from the normal gene pools took the safe option, they stayed home. Then there was us. The Irish Catholics who knew very well from past experiences that when man planned God laughed. Off we went. Sean, Helen, Judy, Stevee and me.

"Peanut butter & jelly. If you don't like it don't eat it."

Mom, I never looked up. I just looked at every step I was putting my feet on. The more steps we climbed, the lighter it got and the harder you could feel the rain. When I reached the top step and looked up, it took my breath away. There standing majestically before me in the distance was the first caisson of the Brooklyn Bridge, a huge American Flag stood atop, waving graciously through the fog and driving rain. I was Dorothy when she first found Oz. I swear I could hear Frank Sinatra belting out New York, New York. I was truly living a dream.

Somebody somewhere must really love me to give me this. It was just like Gra said it was. Wooden planks and all. The rain came down in torrents. No one said a word about it. We had the bridge pretty much to ourselves. I hope you like the toast we made to you guys when we got to the middle of the bridge. I never had champagne on a bridge before. I really thought that those two who came up to us while we were drinking our champagne were going to mug us. Helen squeaks out "You from Seattle?" "Yep." They weren't muggers. Well we made it to the other side. It was just the most incredible thing mom.

"If you don't stop I'll send you back where you came from"

They wanted to walk back across. I couldn't. Not another step. They were kind enough to tell me to get my ass in the wheelchair for the trip back. There was no wind to speak of. On the trip back there was only fog. Mom this was the greatest thing I have ever done in my life. I can't really explain it. It's just something. I can still feel the feeling I had. It was unlike anything I have ever felt before. And you know mom, there's nothing better than laughing your ass off with your family and friends. A lot happened from the time we started our trek across the bridge that day. History was at an optimum that day. Sadly, Pope John Paul died, torrential rains deluged and New Jersey was flooded. Gale force winds bellowed, putting parts of Long Island in the dark, and five, very happy people laughed and reminisced their way into new memories without a hitch.

"What allowance"

I would have asked you to walk across the bridge if you were here. You would have been a perfect tour guide. Stevee did an excellent job. She is quite knowledgeable about the city. If you were here I would have called you from the bridge. I would have told you it was like going back in time. I would have told you how much the stories you and Gra told me about the bridge were still so alive in my heart. I would have told you I loved you, while standing on top of the world. You know mom, I dared myself to live a dream and I was able to share the reality of that daring dream with those who dared to dream too. It was the ultimate gift to life. How cool is that. I am so lucky.

'Didn't I tell you." "if I told you once I told you a hundred times ...."

Your bottle of Jean Nate' is starting to evaporate. No, I did not use it as toilet water, unlike the blue bottle from childhood. I have grown some in the class department. Do they still make that stuff? I wonder, no they say kids are smarter now. Hey, it said toilet water. And you had it on the back of the toilet. No worse than daddy putting hotdogs in the split pea soup.

"twinkle, twinkle little star"

It's hard not to think about you sometimes. Sometimes you just touch down like a whisper. Time has been kind and allowed my broken heart to mend somewhat. I am able to feel the missing with much less pain, but it still seems really big, and at times bigger than I am, if you know what I mean...Do you miss me mom? I just had to ask you that. It's hard for me to ask you that, because I know I drove you nuts. But I never drove you nuts on purpose. It just seemed like that to you. I was your Penance. God

gives everyone one. I have more than one.

"Could I please , no and don't ask me again"

Now that I think about it you had a couple

too. But the missing thing, I was just wondering.

Your missing must be crazy. I only have you to miss;

you have lots of people to miss. Funny thing when I

was a kid and running away all the time I never

missed you. I was too busy trying to figure out where

I was going, how I was going to get there, and what I

was going to do when I got home and you were

indecisive about whether to beat the crap out of me or

not. I remember one time Helen wanted to run away

with me. I wouldn't take her because it was my only

claim to fame and you would have definitely killed

me if I had taken her with me. One time she did come

with me and we took a bus to Hempstead. I

remember one time when the police picked me up and an officer who knew daddy poked his head in the car and said; "wait till you get your rear end home". Some things in life you never forget, this is one of mine.

"Could you please sign my homework". 'Who did your homework?"

There is a silence in my heart that I know is there because you are gone. I knew nothing would feel the same, nothing would look the same, but I never really thought that I as a person would change as I have. I stand taller now, though the extra weight does pull me down. I look at things in more ways than just the usual stubborn Irish "only" way. I cherish what I have, when I find it. I still remember that no matter how bad I think I have it there is still someone out there who has it a lot worse than I do. When I feel like crap I get out of bed and do what I have to do so that I make sure I feel really crappy by mid-day. Then I don't feel guilty when I feel sick enough to die. Washing behind my ears no longer makes me want to get up and go. That was your cure-all for us. Throw us in a tub of warm soapy water, scrub the hell out of our very sensitive Irish skin and send us off. Worked most times except when we were puking all over the rugs. Then it was ginger ale. Hoffman ginger ale. No ice, no gulping, just sips. "The prettiest girl I ever saw was sippin' Hoffman right through a straw."

"Could you please sign this?" What for"? "I was absent"
" When?" all week....

Although the Catholic Church would never recognize the miracles that happened in our house, most people that know us would surely agree that it was a miracle you didn't kill me. Or that you didn't kill any of us including daddy for that matter. In the Harvest moon of my days, I find myself laughing an awful lot about my encounters with your bouts of "I'm going to kill you", look. You never said you were going to kill any us, you just said you were going to break our necks when you caught up with us. When you did catch me I used to think I was better off dead.

"Stick out your tongue. It's black you're lying to me."

Daddy was always going to "tan our behinds" when he caught us. But we knew he never would, because he was too lazy to get off the couch to chase us. Although, when daddy's eyes used to water you knew you were soon in deep doo doo. They didn't often water but when they did, look out. It usually happened when we sat down to attempt a family dinner.

"Don't lean back on your chair you're gonna break your neck" "Sit up straight" "Get your elbows off the table". "Stop picking at the meat" "I want that plate how come she always gets that plate"? "Damn it I told you to stop leaning back on your chair". "Is there anymore milk"? "Can I have some 'ore" "Wait till daddy gets some". CRASH, silverware clinking, tablecloth just slid to the left side of the table by a foot. All eyes look to the side of the table where daddy is looking towards the floor and stare in silence, waiting to bust in laughter. "What'd I tell ya"! " Didn't I tell you not to lean back on your chair, now, get up here and sit right and eat." "Damn it I get more peace at work from a bunch of strangers." This is daddy's exit to the back porch to

watch the Munster's and lay on the couch. You
stayed for a little more punishment.

"Stop picking at your food".

It was worse when we had a guest for dinner.
Everyone would want the guest to sit next to him or
her. Once the fight was over about where the guest
would sit, the next loud noise was your saying
"Guests first". Even daddy listened when you said
that, although he usually carved and ate his share of
the meat while in the kitchen. Daddy always got the
little leg on the end of the leg of lamb. Daddy always
got the end of the meatloaf. Daddy always got the
drumstick. He always got the crispy stuff from the
macaroni and cheese and thank Jesus he was the one
who loved White Castle. I remember one time he sent
me in there for an order of fifty hamburgers. I
whispered to the lady behind the counter that I

wanted fifty hamburgers. I was mortified that I was the one that had to do this. Nobody ever really bought that many hamburgers, not a little kid anyway. The lady promptly yells, "I need fifty burgers, will everyone behind her please move to the front counter." I suddenly had the inclination to want to die. People were looking at me like "whadda ya kiddin". I stare painfully at the sign that tells you to "buy em by the sack". I left with five sacks that day. Daddy was happy. He ate some on the way home, treated his kids and then some on less then four dollars. What a treat.

"Where were you?"

The best treat was when we were real little and poked out the holes in the side of the burger holders to make it look like the castle had windows. I can't remember my phone number but I can remember giving an empty White Castle box, air conditioning. I think that was a daddy thing. Just like the peanut with Santa Claus inside. I still try and open peanuts when I get a whole one to see if I still see Santa Claus. Yep, every once in a while I get lucky and I look at a peanut just right. I can see his beard lying on the sleigh and his face as plain as day. You and daddy didn't have much to give us in the way of bikes, cars and stereos. What you did give us colors a lot of worlds, with a lot of laughter. Not mean laughter, but funny laughter. Laughter that always makes you laugh even harder. Sometimes it wasn't funny when it was happening, but later on when you found you were still alive, someone always made a funny about whatever.., and we cried laughing.

"Use soap when you wash your hands"

Sean and I were debating who was responsible for Humphrey the rabbit's sudden departure from our lives. I always thought it was you who stepped on his tail. I remember you screaming and looking down on the porch floor at a white ball of fur. I could have sworn you stepped on his tail. He hopped, his tail stayed under your toes and we never saw him again. The way you screamed and then the way you stopped dead in your tracks, I could have sworn you did it. I guess you did get blamed for everything. It doesn't really matter who did it. The questions in my mind have always been, did his tail ever grow back, and where did he go.

"Where's your mother".

Remember when Helen's gold fish died and we had the funeral. The fish got buried in a little jewelry box in the backayard. Someone dug that up. Of course there were the little baby ducks that daddy brought home from the 62-63 World's Fair. They used to have an incubator over there and he would bring home the chicks once they hatched, totally to your dismay. You made us take them out in the backayard. We built swimming pools and diving boards which sadly the latter of the two, most ducks don't use. Most of them fell and broke their necks. Or just died from neglect. You have very fertile soil in your backyard. If I were to stand there now, I could tell you where Prince the dog was buried, where the ducks met their demise, and where our first big dig to China took place. I think there's still a bit of a slope where that was. We could never get all the dirt back in the hole. If I were to stand there right now at this very moment in time, I would ask God to let me stand there with you. Just for a single precious moment of time. Just because.

"Mooooooooom he's got my good shirt on".

I've been thinking mom, you know when you're born, someone feeds you, teaches you to walk. She cries when you go off to kindergarten (or jumps for joy). She watches as you learn to ride your bike. She spends what seems to be billions of hours teaching you to hopefully become a lady or a gentleman, but nobody teaches you how to get by without the one who brought you into the world. Sure mothers leave expectedly and unexpectedly just like others in your life, but when she leaves you, you never forget that she's gone. There's always an instant that you stop and think of them, unlike the way you stop to think of others. It always seems like people have a look of wonder about them, when they think of their moms. Through birth, she is there with you. With any blessed luck you have her to haunt until it's time for you to show her, what you've learned. It's when you can't show her or call her anymore, which brings you through an abyss of wonder, in your heart and mind. Mom, you never told me what to do when you left. You never told me about the emptiness. You never told me about the silence. Yes, you told me the crap would fly, but you never told me what would happen to my world once you were no longer in it. I suppose the biggest thing was that I have no place to call "home" anymore. I have no one to stick up for me the way only you could. There's no one to protect me, to keep me safe like you did. You were the last person on this earth that I looked up to. Now everyone is the same. I hadn't lived in your house for thirty some odd years, but it was always home and you and daddy were always my mother and father. Now the house is someone else's, and you and dad are pictures and knick-knacks collecting dust in my apartment. Funny how life happens.

"Somebody let the dog out"

I have tried on numerous occasions to run away since you left. It hasn't worked. Not just because I can't run literally, but because it just wouldn't be the same without you. There's no one to stand at the front door with that look of "Thank God she's home now I'm going to kill her " look. There's no one to give me the silent treatment for 2 days then get me the reflectors I always wanted for my bike. Besides, there's nowhere to go. The places you use to look for me are long ago memories drifting in time. Gra's not here to give me those peanut butter cheese crackers. Remember that one mom? I walked from Valley Stream to Long Beach. I remember wanting to turn back but it seemed like it was to far to go back. I

94

could run anywhere now you know. Having a car in which everything works, is a perfect run away. And I could go really far away and you could never catch me…. How sad is that…

"Where's your father?"

As I write you this letter, I sometimes imagine a glimpse of you within its pages. Your unforgettable smile, the awesome beauty of your Irish expression. Then I sometimes see you chasing me with the "you're dead when I catch you look". I see you lighting that old kitchen oven to keep us warm on cold winter days. There's so much to see mom, it's like being in a gallery. There's some Rockwell, there's some Lally black and white, there's even a beauty that eludes my ability to describe. That's the one that's yours and mine. No one has seen what we had. No one could ever understand where we went. Nor could they ever conceive what we did. It is so sweet, so very delicate. It comes to me every so often. It touches me softly, feather like. It captures my being and a rapture of peace settles within me. I see you shaking your head! I know you know what I mean. Whatever happened back then brought me to where I am, and to where I believe God has taken you. You have reached everlasting peace and I was blessed to have witnessed it. There is nothing more as your child I could wish for you. There was never a time in my life that I amassed such strength as when I watched you go. I never, ever remember feeling such peace as I did when you slipped away ever so gently. Thank you for being my mother even in the end and always.

"Did anyone feed the dog?"

Sometimes I wish I could blink you back just for a little while. Just so you could sew my jeans, make spaghetti, yell at me or just need me for something. You became so much like your own mother towards the very end. You really laughed, and when you cried you really cried making me totally like a Gumby. When Gra cried I would look at those baby blues and want to die. When I watched you cry and saw those tears fall carelessly down your beautiful face I was paralyzed with fear. There's nothing worse than seeing your mother cry, well except if you're the reason she's crying. I was never quite sure what to do when you cried. I'm still not sure. Lifetimes ago, you didn't cry that much and if you did we hi-tailed it somewhere safer than where you were standing. It was usually one of us who caused you to cry. But in the end when you cried I hoped it wasn't something any of us had done. I had hoped that it was God nudging you along, and you refusing to be nudged. I think that it was giving up life as you had come to know it. You did that in your own time in your own way. As we got closer to the end you cried less and I cried more. It was like the bigger things that you had to let go of, the smaller I began to feel, and it seemed the braver you got. It truly was an amazing journey.

"Where's the top to the sugar bowl, we're gonna get ants"

Since I took the journey with you I find myself watching where I'm going. There is not much that I take for granted. I think the accident took care of that. But I think our journey together brought the fuzzy stuff more into focus. It's been ten years since that day I was sitting in the back seat of George's car and someone running a red light broadsided us. It has been that long since Dad and you made the trip, every weekend up to Connecticut to see me. And amazingly it has been that long since the family found out I had a brain and that it was damaged. The person I was died that day. The woman who would move the piano for you, who raked the leaves, and fixed your car was gone. I was different now. I spent a year and then some learning to do what should have come naturally. And then I got mad. And then I went from a wheelchair, back to driving a car within three years. There was no stopping me. I would never be the way I was before. But I would still have a heart and soul. Most important was that I had the survival instincts that you had instilled in me. The instincts you used to raise the brood and daddy. No matter what, you always got back up till something else came along and knocked you back down. Just like Wyle E. Coyote who happens to be my hero.

I know you never fully accepted what happened to me. As a parent when one of your "normal" ducks breaks a wing, you still try and get them to swim. After a while you accepted my floating. You never made a deal out of helping me. When we were out, and were having a "must be cut to consume" dinner you just took my plate, cut everything up and gave it back, never saying a word. When we walked, you always waited till I got down the curb and then you'd put your arm through mine and walk me across the street. I can still feel the warmth I used feel when you did that. And I still remember always having to pull you back because there was a car coming. You always brought back my cane when a kid decided to see what it was like to use one and forgot to give it back.

There was a kindness in your not asking or

talking about it. I really didn't want to talk about it,

mostly because I still really had no idea what

happened except that I banged my head and broke

most of my main working parts. I know it sounds

funny, but I really have no idea what happened.

There was no sound, no feeling. No anything. I don't

remember anything. I remember making myself

crazy trying to remember what had happened. Just

so that I could know why, I was now the way I was. I

must have banged my head a million times, and

nothing happened to me. I guess this was the BIG

BANG. What I do remember is not being able to do

much of anything. Friends remember more than I do.

And sometimes when I piss them off they are more

than happy to tell me where I was and where I am

now, and if I don't cut the crap they will gladly send

101

me back to where I was. Friends are wonderful. Sometimes they can shake your tree more than a parent.

"He went fishin'."

Without whatever it was that you taught me, I never would have gotten to this point without it. I'm not sure all the time about stubbornness, no self-pity or the starving in Europe thing. I can look down the street and see hungry people. Having no self-pity keeps me from knowing if there really is something wrong with me and the stubbornness, well that has caused me to be creative in telling people to go to hell and have a good time on the way. I attribute all of this to my Irish heritage, the school of wooden spoon and a love and respect for you and dad. I know because of you and dad I can stand tall in times of adversity. I can come up with a quick fix for most things although I do spend a great deal of time later on trying to get out of my quick fix. But I am still here. It's a mystery to me and some others how I am, but I am. I was not able to watch the "movie" of my life until I was old enough to know how hard it was for you and dad raising all of us in the 50's 60's 70's and some of the 80's. Yes it was that long for some. When I was smart enough to understand that part of growing up is never forgetting where you came from, and never being ashamed of it, I watched the "movie" over and over. It would become the greatest education of my life. Thank you for never giving up.

"How many times do I have to tell you not to play ball in the house"

I wish with all my heart that you were here. I said it once and I will say it again, when your mother leaves for other pastures, part of you leaves with her. The child in me that ran to you when they shot the man out of the cannon at the circus. The child in me that ran to you when I broke my nose climbing over the back fence. The child in me who ran from your wooden spoon. The child in me who hated going to the A&P with you. The child in me who laughed when you went to sit on the hassock and missed. The child in me, who ran away eons of times, from you, wasn't the part of me that left with you. Nor was it the woman that you allowed to comfort you so many times towards the end.

"Hang up your coat"

I am still comforting you. It was an entire part of my person that left with you. This part of me has tried to learn the hardest healing that I will never feel again in my life. First it was an actual physical pain. My heart was broken. Then it was emptiness. There was nowhere to go to ease the missing. Everywhere I looked it was there. Emptiness. The part of my person that left with you was the part that loved you with all my heart. The familiar part of me that was connected to you. And the familiar part of you that was quite successful in trying to connect with me. The physical connection. Connected through birth. And a wooden spoon. Now I cherish dearly the years of testing the waters, and the moments that are etched in my soul with laughter. There they will remain until I die.

"Mom the fish are floating again"

The first five miles of life without you have slipped through my tear-laden fingers. It has not been an oh she's gone I'll be all right kind of road trip. I have looked at every moment I have had since you left, and wondered where to put it. I suppose it's all part of growing through the weeds. I have never in my life, ever looked at things as I do now. There is no hurry for anything. Although I do not read text as often as I should, I do take time to look at everything as if I were reading its résumé. It fascinates me how in moments, zillions of things happen. In my moments I do not let the zillions of things take over. Rather, I do what feels to be at that moment. I have learned to trust myself. That came out going down that incredible road with you. The road that took us to never- ever-land. You and I both proved our strength. You did it by doing the whole shebang in your own way. You did it just the way you wanted. I did it by never letting go. I couldn't hear or see anything, except the moment we were in. I tried to never let fear over power my need to do whatever I could do for you. And mom sometimes that feared seemed heavier than the piano. Out of that fear came this woman who I am now. I make sense most times now, so much so I scare the bejesus out of myself. I suppose part of that was finding my sense of self. It was always there, it just needed to come out, without pre-judgment or conflict. I believe all those thoughts, became things, because I journeyed with you. There was a reason you were stuck with me to the very end. Thank you.

"Drink out of a glass"

I am not afraid of life anymore. Although I am still afraid of thunder and lightening, I am no longer wondering about tomorrows. They will continue to come first light of the day no matter what. I do wonder where the hell am I once in a while, but I am not afraid. I attribute that to you, old friends, new friends and banging my head. I can't move fast enough to be afraid. Fear causes flight. I am in the Emus status as far as flight goes. My old friends stuck by me through my adjustment without you and new found friends offered friendship, laughter and kindness. I am so lucky.

"Collection money is for church, not candy"

Tell me mom, do you have assigned seats at the great table where you now sit with others who have passed into memories. Are you allowed to put your elbows on the table, lean back on your chair and open you mouth when it's full of the evening's dinner? Do you laugh a lot about the day's events and wonder who's got the dishes? I have visions that you all sit there with a lot of class and it's peaceful. I have visions of your beautiful smile peeking down to see what's going on under the table. I am still allowed to dream and have you in my dreams. I know when time covers over much of the trodden path I will begin to say, " My mother used to"… or "I remember when my mother would"…. But for now I am still gathering the things to remember. I am just not ready to past tense you, with any absolute yet. No I don't think it's any kind of abnormal mourning. Just a wee bit of healing. I mourned you while you were still here. I mourned you, as you stopped doing things, like when you stopped driving, making coffee and eating. I mourned the day you told me the cancer was b ack. It was the beginning of the end, and I couldn't help but mourn. Reality was right there. We really were faced with the fact that we had no control with what was happening. It's a good thing most people don't wish to face reality. The blow is deafening.

"Stop playing with your food"

You know mom, I have come to know just how very fragile, life is. Through my own experiences and my walk with you I look at things much differently now. There's nothing more important, than the sunrise. What happens in between the rising and setting sun is a gift.

"Did you clean your room?"

By the way mom, you left with the name of my childhood imaginary friend. I have no idea of its name but you remembered it always. Is there anyway you could send it to me? I think it had an inky to it, but then, every kid who can't speak says inky. Peace.

Love,

Mary

P.S. I am sorry we didn't Irish Wake you. I guess
they sort of did, but not like it should have been. It
should have been in your house, where for eons of
times before, Irish or not we had an Irish wake for the
dearly departed. Whether they were family or not.
You of all people deserved an Irish Wake. We should
have laughed in your dinning room and your kitchen
and sat quietly in the living room. The glasses in the
china closet should have shook once again. We
should have put your refrigerator through the
ultimate punishment. Your Irish wake happened in
the minds and hearts of the ones who knew better.

I have covered much ground since you left. I
can't remember all of it, but I promise I am not
allowing your legacy to pass on by just collecting
dust. People know you were here. They know that
against incredible odds you set the stage for a VFW

111

full of Family. You have enough college graduates

now to fill the dining room.

Your death and my mourning you has been

such an incredible experience. I thought the world

stopped when you died, but it didn't. Everything in

my little world just stopped and I begged of the world

the same. How could there be movement. You were

stilled. The woman who fought with every inch of her

soul was stilled. My mother was gone. At first I

thought everything was in slow motion. I am so

grateful that Sean and I had those last moments with

you. No one deserved to be with you more than him

and I. Just the three of us in total peace saying

farewell to the anthology of our lives.

I lost more than you on that day. I also lost the

pin that held me together with the others. In your

death came the honest outcome of who we all really

were and are. I have learned since then that because

112

you're family the intent to hurt has no bounds. They think you'll keep coming back. Now that you're gone no one has to go back anymore. No more pretending to be civil to each other. No more lies.

The sun from the East is higher now. Your old half dead cherry tree must be getting ready to bloom. I don't even know if it's still there. I don't know if there are half a dozen kids in 100% cotton white anklets, traipsing, sneaker-less through the blanket of blossoms or wayward cherries. I don't know if they are walking through the house and putting their feet up on the couch. They could never do it like we did it. I like my memory of the cherry blossoms. I liked the fact that your father planted that tree, just for you. All the years I brought cherry juice through the house I never knew that.

It is such a newborn spring day as I sit and finish this letter to you. Life has been good to me. I

113

try desperately to be good to life. It is not always easy. Raising me is difficult. I don't know how you raised seven others and me. I'm making myself nuts. Anyway, there will always be something everywhere to keep the memory of you alive in me. As I age ungraciously I laugh at how much I am becoming you. Or how much of you I was and try to change it. Not that there were things so bad that they needed change, but I learned some by seeing. You have no idea what kind of strength you left me. You traveled the most ultimately feared journey of life: the reality death sentence. All those days that you woke up you knew that you were dying. And there was not a thing you could do about it. The average person doesn't get up in the morning with that thought on their mind. They get up and go through the motions. Thank you for showing me the fragile side of life. It has allowed me to treat life as such. It has given me a freedom that I have never known before. As I told you before I am not afraid anymore. The worst fear of my entire life happened. Losing you.

I wish it hadn't taken your leaving for this to happen. But I suppose it's all part of it. Losing, growing, knowing. God gives and God takes away. Sure death is a part of life. It is what happens in between the living and the dying that one must take the time to hear, to feel, and to cherish. On my living into dying journey with you I had a lifetime. I became what a daughter only gets one chance to become. Motherly, to her own. I tucked you in. I attempted to cook for you. I sat on the top step, until you fell asleep. I turned out the light, and kissed your forehead. Somewhere, between the living and the dying the child in the daughter, took refuge elsewhere. A woman came about. And I would do everything in my power to keep you safe. Hey Who Knew.

Wherever it is now that I am, it's pretty precious. I am not afraid to count my blessings aloud. I still laugh at myself a hundred times a day and I still scare the beJesus out of myself when I'm not looking. But mostly mom I'm trying. For me that's half the battle. I am so very proud of you for all you did here in your mortal life. I am sorry it took so long for me to understand some of the things you did and why you did them. But I was a kid then and I was not supposed to understand. I was supposed to contribute to your insanity. I think I did a damn good job.

I know you aren't quite sure what it is I am doing here since you left. I am not raising eight kids, nor do I have any under foot. By the way you missed your first great-grand children by a couple of days. There's no stopping them now. Thanks be to God. As for me, I'm doing what I can when I can, proving there's nothing on this earth like stubborn Irish.

Sometimes in the days that pass by I catch myself

calling myself "my mothers daughter". Damn

proudly I might add. From you, dad and Gra, I carry

an arsenal of survival tactics: stubbornness, humor,

wit, kindness, compassion and my faith. My favorite

of course is never having any money. I will never be

anything great except being your daughter, and mom

that is the greatest. Peace... ... ...

Love Always,

Mary

ISBN 141209708-8

9 781412 097086